Unique
Baby Names

Unique Baby Names

by
Laverne Condappa-Ward

It's a Boy!

Children are special
A blessing from above
With names that are chosen
As an expression of love!

Introduction

In this book you will find a compilation of unique baby names to consider when naming your newborn. It contains a wide range of options to give your child a name that stands out. These unique names are from various cultures, regions, and languages, including traditional and modern options. It also lists the meanings and origins of these names, making it easier for you to choose a name that resonates with your family's heritage, values, or aspirations.

In addition, this book provides you with inspiration to find an uncommon and distinctive name for your little one. By exploring the variety of options, you can find a name that feels special and meaningful for you and your child.

Overall, this unique baby name book is an excellent resource for you to find a distinctive name that reflects your child's individuality and uniqueness.

Baby Names Beginning with "A"

Names for Girls

1. Azura - Latin, meaning "sky blue"
2. Astrid - Scandinavian, meaning "divinely beautiful" or "fair goddess"
3. Amara - Greek, meaning "eternal" or "unfading"
4. Adira - Hebrew, meaning "strong" or "noble"
5. Anwen - Welsh, meaning "fair" or "blessed"
6. Adalwolfa - German, meaning "noble wolf"
7. Asherah - Hebrew, meaning "she who walks in the sea"
8. Althea - Greek, meaning "healer" or "whole"
9. Adalira - German, meaning "noble" or "kind"
10. Ailani - Hawaiian, meaning "chief" or "leader"

Names for Boys

1. Axl - Scandinavian, meaning "father of peace"
2. Alder - English, meaning "old" or "wise"
3. Aric - Germanic, meaning "ruler of all" or "eternal ruler"
4. Aziz - Arabic, meaning "powerful" or "beloved"
5. Aubrey - French, meaning "fair ruler"
6. Arlo - English, meaning "fortified hill"
7. Arden - English, meaning "valley of the eagle"
8. Anson - English, meaning "son of Anne"
9. Atlas - Greek, meaning "enduring" or "strong"
10. Anson - English, meaning "son of Anne"

Baby Names Beginning with "B"

Names for Girls

1. Beau - French, meaning "handsome" or "attractive"
2. Brigette - Norse, meaning "exalted one"
3. Blythe - Old English, meaning "happy" or "joyful"
4. Braelynn - Irish, meaning "freckled" or "princess"
5. Brynn - Welsh, meaning "hill" or "fair, pretty"
6. Belva - Latin, meaning "lovely" or "pretty"
7. Beryl - Greek, meaning "precious gemstone"
8. Bardot - French, meaning "good shooting"
9. Brennagh - Irish, meaning "fair" or "fair-haired"
10. Bexley -English, meaning "place where box trees grow"

Names for Boys

1. Boston - English, meaning "from the town of Boston"
2. Bjorn - Scandinavian, meaning "bear"
3. Bowie - Scottish, meaning "blond"
4. Barret - English, meaning "fair-haired" or "arrow"
5. Beckett - English, meaning "stream" or "brook"
6. Balthazar - Aramaic, meaning "Baal protect the king"
7. Bran - Welsh, meaning "raven"
8. Blaze - English, meaning "flame"
9. Breckin - Welsh, meaning "freckled"
10. Boris - Slavic, meaning "fighter" or "short"

Baby Names Beginning with "C"

Names for Girls

1. Calantha - Greek, meaning "beautiful flower"
2. Celeste - Latin, meaning "heavenly" or "of the sky"
3. Calliope - Greek, meaning "beautiful voice"
4. Cyra - Greek, meaning "lord" or "ruler"
5. Cordelia - Latin, meaning "heart" or "child of the sea"
6. Cora - Greek, meaning "maiden" or "girl"
7. Celia - Latin, meaning "heavenly" or "of the sky"
8. Camilla - Latin, meaning "young ceremonial attendant"
9. Cytheria - Greek, meaning "born of Venus" (the goddess of love)
10. Carina - Latin, meaning "beloved" or "dear one"

Names for Boys

1. Caius - Latin, meaning "rejoice"
2. Cormac - Irish, meaning "son of the charioteer"
3. Calloway - Scottish, meaning "from the forest by the water"
4. Cyprian - Greek, meaning "from Cyprus"
5. Caleb - Hebrew, meaning "faithful, devotion, whole-hearted"
6. Cruz - Spanish, meaning "cross" or "the passion of Christ"
7. Cosimo - Italian, meaning "order" or "universe"
8. Cyler - English, meaning "one who lives by the sea"
9. Caspian - Persian, meaning "from the Caspian Sea region"
10. Conall - Irish, meaning "strong wolf"

Baby Names Beginning with "D"

Names for Girls

1. Della – English, meaning "noble"
2. Dania – Arabic, meaning "close" or "near"
3. Dakota - Native American, meaning "friend" or "ally"
4. Davina – Scottish, meaning "beloved"
5. Darlene – English, meaning "darling"
6. Dora – Greek, meaning "gift"
7. Darcie – French, meaning "dark"
8. Diamantina – Greek, meaning "diamond"
9. Desdemona – Greek, meaning "unlucky"
10. Danika – Slavic, meaning "morning star"

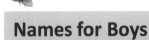

Names for Boys

1. Declan – Irish, meaning "full of goodness"
2. Dante – Italian, meaning "enduring"
3. Darian – Persian, meaning "maintaining possession"
4. Dax – French, meaning "leader"
5. Denver – English, meaning "green valley"
6. Deshawn – American, meaning "from the southern tribe"
7. Dorian – Greek, meaning "of the Dorian tribe"
8. Drake – English, meaning "dragon"
9. Darnell – English, meaning "hidden nook"
10. Dario – Italian, meaning "possessing wealth"

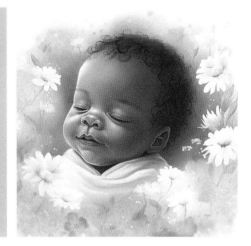

Baby Names Beginning with "E"

Names for Girls

1. Elodie – French, meaning "foreign riches"
2. Elinor – Greek, meaning "bright, shining light"
3. Esme – French, meaning "beloved"
4. Emmeline – German, meaning "hardworking"
5. Eloise – French, meaning "famous in war"
6. Evangeline – Greek, meaning "bringer of good news"
7. Elspeth – Scottish, meaning "God is my oath"
8. Eira – Welsh, meaning "snow"
9. Eadlyn – English, meaning "noble"
10. Eleonora – Greek, meaning "bright one"

Names for Boys

1. Easton – English, meaning "from the eastern settlement"
2. Ellis – Welsh, meaning "kind"
3. Emmett – German, meaning "powerful"
4. Ezra – Hebrew, meaning "helper"
5. Eamon – Irish, meaning "wealthy protector"
6. Elijah – Hebrew, meaning "my God is Yahweh"
7. Eastwood – English, meaning "from the east forest"
8. Everett – English, meaning "brave as a wild boar"
9. Ellisdon – English, meaning "from the nobleman's hill"
10. Errol – Scottish, meaning "nobleman"

Baby Names Beginning with "F"

Names for Girls

1. Felicity – Latin, meaning "happiness"
2. Freya – Norse, meaning "lady"
3. Flora – Latin, meaning "flower"
4. Freda – German, meaning "peaceful ruler"
5. Fallon – Irish, meaning "leader"
6. Frida – Scandinavian, meaning "peaceful"
7. Freja – Scandinavian, meaning "lady"
8. Felicia – Latin, meaning "lucky"
9. Felipa – Spanish, meaning "lover of horses"
10. Fae – Scottish, meaning "fairy"

Names for Boys

1. Finn – Irish, meaning "fair" or "white"
2. Fletcher – English, meaning "arrow maker"
3. Finnick – English, meaning "handsome"
4. Forrest – English, meaning "dweller in the woods"
5. Frank – German, meaning "free man"
6. Felix – Latin, meaning "lucky" or "successful"
7. Finnbar – Irish, meaning "fair-haired"
8. Ford – English, meaning "river crossing"
9. Falco – Italian, meaning "falcon"
10. Fintan – Irish, meaning "little fair one"

Baby Names Beginning with "G"

Names for Girls

1. Gia - Italian name meaning "God is gracious"
2. Gwendolyn - Welsh name meaning "white ring"
3. Galen - Greek name meaning "calm"
4. Genevieve - French name meaning "white wave"
5. Ginevra - Italian name meaning "white as a juniper"
6. Giselle - French name meaning "pledge"
7. Ginebra - Spanish name meaning "white as foam"
8. Ginevra - Italian name meaning "white as a juniper"
9. Gala - Spanish name meaning "festive"
10. Gloriana - Latin name meaning "glorious"

Names for Boys

1. Gage - English name meaning "oath"
2. Graham - Scottish name meaning "gravelly homestead"
3. Gareth - Welsh name meaning "gentle"
4. Greer - Scottish name meaning "watchful"
5. Grant - English name meaning "great"
6. Garrick - English name meaning "ruler of the spear"
7. Gentry - English name meaning "gentleman"
8. Gaven - Scottish name meaning "white hawk"
9. Gio - Italian name meaning "God is gracious"
10. Galen - Greek name meaning "calm"

Baby Names Beginning with "H"

Names for Girls

1. Harper - English name meaning "harp player"
2. Hadley - English name meaning "heather meadow"
3. Hadiya - Arabic name meaning "gift"
4. Heidi – German name meaning "noble"
5. Hira - Arabic name meaning "shining"
6. Harriet - English name meaning "ruler of the home"
7. Hana - Japanese name meaning "flower"
8. Halima - Arabic name meaning "gentle"
9. Hailey - English name meaning "field of hay"
10. Haruka - Japanese name meaning "far away"

Names for Boys

1. Holden - English name meaning "gracious holder"
2. Harlow - English name meaning "army hill"
3. Harrison - English name meaning "son of Harry"
4. Hayes - English name meaning "at the hedged area"
5. Hudson - English name meaning "son of Hugh"
6. Hunter - English name meaning "one who hunts"
7. Hendrix - English name meaning "son of Henry"
8. Hugo - German name meaning "mind" or "spirit"
9. Holt - English name meaning "woodland"
10. Hamish - Scottish name meaning "supplanter"

Baby Names Beginning with "I"

Names for Girls

1. Isadora - Greek name meaning "gift of Isis"
2. Imogen - Irish name meaning "maiden"
3. Indira - Hindi name meaning "beauty"
4. Isolde - Welsh name meaning "fair lady"
5. Isla - Scottish name meaning "island"
6. Ivanna - Russian name meaning "God is gracious"
7. Imogen - Irish name meaning "maiden"
8. Isabella - Hebrew name meaning "God is my oath"
9. Isolde - Welsh name meaning "fair lady"
10. Ivanna - Russian name meaning "God is gracious"

Names for Boys

1. Idris - Welsh name meaning "fiery Lord"
2. Ignatius - Latin name meaning "fiery one"
3. Iker - Basque name meaning "visitation"
4. Ilan - Hebrew name meaning "tree"
5. Immanuel - Hebrew name meaning "God is with us"
6. Ismael - Arabic name meaning "God will hear"
7. Ivan - Russian name meaning "God is gracious"
8. Iver - Scandinavian name meaning "yew wood"
9. Inigo - Spanish name meaning "fiery"
10. Isidore - Greek name meaning "gift of Isis"

Baby Names Beginning with "J"

Names for Girls

1. Jocasta – Greek, meaning "Shining moon"
2. Joline – Hebrew, meaning "Jehovah increases".
3. Jorja – English, it is a variant of the name Georgia, which means "farmer"
4. Josslyn: American, it is a combination of the names Joss and Lyn
5. Jovanka: Slavic, it is a combination of the names Jovana and Janka
6. Jovita: Spanish, meaning "full of life" or "healthy."
7. Julliana: American , it is a combination of the names Jullia and Ana
8. Juniper: English, it is a type of evergreen tree known for its small blue-grey berries.
9. Justina: Latin, meaning "just" or "fair."
10. Jyoti: Indian, meaning "light" or "flame"

Names for Boys

1. Jasper - Persian name meaning "treasurer"
2. Julian - Latin name meaning "youthful"
3. Jagger - English name meaning "one who carries a pack"
4. Jaxon - English name meaning "son of Jack"
5. Jett - English name meaning "jet black"
6. Judson - English name meaning "son of Judd"
7. Jackson - English name meaning "son of Jack"
8. Joel - Hebrew name meaning "Jehovah is God"
9. Justin - Latin name meaning "just upright"
10. Jensen - Scandinavian name meaning "son of Jens"

Baby Names Beginning with "K"

Names for Girls

1. Kaida – Japanese, meaning "Little dragon" or "Loveable"
2. Kalila - Arabic, meaning "dear one" or "beloved."
3. Kamali – Indian, meaning "young and beautiful"
4. Karmen – Spanish, meaning "song" or "poem."
5. Karyna - Ukrainian, it is a variant of the name Katherine, meaning "pure" or "clear."
6. Kaveri - Indian, it is the name of a river in South India, it also means "poetess."
7. Keiko - Japanese, meaning "blessed child" or "happy child."
8. Kelis - Greek, meaning "courier" or "messenger."
9. Kenzi - American, it is a combination of the names Ken and Zoe
10. Khushi - Indian, meaning "happiness" or "joy."

Names for Boys

1. Kellen – Irish, meaning "slender"
2. Kael – Irish, meaning "fair and slender"
3. Kian – Irish, meaning "gracious gift of God"
4. Kendrick – English, meaning "bold ruler"
5. Kellan – Irish, meaning "bright-headed"
6. Kai – Hawaiian, meaning "sea"
7. Kato – African, meaning "the second-born"
8. Kace – English, meaning "alert, watchful"
9. Kadeem – Arabic, meaning "servant of the generous one"
10. Kameron – Scottish, meaning "crooked nose"

Baby Names Beginning with "L"

Names for Girls

1. Lailah: Arabic, meaning "night" or "born at night."
2. Landon: English, meaning "long hill" or "ridge."
3. Lareina - Spanish, meaning "queen" or "royal one."
4. Larina - Russian, it is a variant of the name Larissa, meaning "citadel" or "fortress."
5. Lavender – English, it is a flower known for its purple colour and fragrant smell.
6. Leila – Arabic, meaning "night" or "dark beauty."
7. Leilani: Hawaiian, meaning "heavenly flower" or "royal child."
8. Lelia - Greek, meaning "light" or "torch."
9. Lenna - English, it is a variant of the name Helen, meaning "light" or "bright one."
10. Leola – German, meaning "lion" or "brave."

Names for Boys

1. Landon - English name meaning "long hill"
2. Liam - Irish name meaning "strong-willed warrior"
3. Leo – Latin, meaning "lion"
4. Lionel - French name meaning "young lion"
5. Lincoln - English name meaning "town by the pool"
6. Landon - English name meaning "long hill"
7. Lance - French name meaning "land"
8. Leif - Norse name meaning "beloved"
9. Lucian – Latin, meaning "light"
10. Logan - Scottish name meaning "small hollow"

Baby Names Beginning with "M"

Names for Girls
1. Maya - Hebrew, meaning "water"
2. Madeline - French, meaning "woman from Magdala"
3. Morgan - Welsh, meaning "circling sea"
4. Mabel - Latin, meaning "lovable"
5. Marissa - Latin, meaning "of the sea"
6. Mila - Slavic, meaning "gracious" or "dear"
7. Margot - French, meaning "pearl"
8. Melody - Greek, meaning "song"
9. Monroe - Scottish, meaning "mouth of the river Roe"
10. Mira - Sanskrit, meaning "wonderful" or "prosperous"

Names for Boys
1. Mason - English name meaning "worker in stone"
2. Maximus – Latin, meaning "greatest"
3. Maverick - English name meaning "independent"
4. Maurice – Latin, meaning "dark-skinned"
5. Max – Latin, meaning "greatest"
6. Myles - Greek name meaning "soldier"
7. Montgomery - English name meaning "Gathering hill"
8. Marley - English name meaning "pleasant wood"
9. Maxwell - Scottish name meaning "great spring"
10. Mitchell - English name meaning "who is like God"

Baby Names Beginning with "N"

Names for Girls

1. Nora - Irish, meaning "light"
2. Nadia - Russian, meaning "hope"
3. Nevaeh - American, meaning "heaven" spelled backwards
4. Niamh - Irish, meaning "radiant" or "bright"
5. Nova - Latin, meaning "new"
6. Nyla - Arabic, meaning "winner" or "success"
7. Nalani - Hawaiian, meaning "calm skies" or "serenity of heaven"
8. Naima - Arabic, meaning "graceful" or "pleasant"
9. Nia - Swahili, meaning "purpose"
10. Nuru - Swahili, meaning "light" or "enlightened"

Names for Boys

1. Nolan - Irish name meaning "famous" or "noble"
2. Noah - Hebrew name meaning "rest, comfort"
3. Nathaniel - Hebrew name meaning "gift of God"
4. Neil - Irish name meaning "champion"
5. Nicodemus - Greek name meaning "victory of the people"
6. Nial - Irish name meaning "champion"
7. Nils - Scandinavian name meaning "victorious people"
8. Nolan - Irish name meaning "famous" or "noble"
9. Nyle - English name meaning "from the island"
10. Norris - English name meaning "from the north"

Baby Names Beginning with "O"

Names for Girls

1. Odette - French, meaning "wealthy"
2. Octavia - Latin, meaning "eighth"
3. Opal - Sanskrit, meaning "precious stone"
4. Orla - Irish, meaning "golden princess"
5. Oriana - Latin, meaning "dawn"
6. Olena - Ukrainian, meaning "torch"
7. Ona - Lithuanian, meaning "gracious" or "full of grace"
8. Oceane - French, meaning "ocean"
9. Omolara – African (Yoruba), meaning "a child is family"
10. Osanna - Hebrew, meaning "deliver us"

Names for Boys

1. Orion - Greek name meaning "son of fire"
2. Oscar - Irish name meaning "deer lover"
3. Oliver - Latin name meaning "olive tree"
4. Owen - Welsh name meaning "young warrior" or "well-born son"
5. Osbert - Anglo-Saxon name meaning "divine brightness"
6. Orville - French name meaning "golden city"
7. Orin - English name meaning "mountain of strength"
8. Otto - German name meaning "wealth" or "fortune"
9. Olu – Nigerian Yoruba name meaning "God" or "ruler"
10. Oumar - Arabic name meaning "long-lived"

Baby Names Beginning with "P"

Names for Girls
1. Piper - English, meaning "flute player"
2. Poppy - Latin, after the Poppy flower
3. Paloma - Spanish, meaning "dove"
4. Priya - Sanskrit, meaning "beloved"
5. Petra - Greek, meaning "rock"
6. Pili - Swahili, meaning "second born"
7. Penda - African, meaning "beloved"
8. Princess - English, meaning "royal daughter"
9. Paige - English, meaning "young assistant"
10. Prunella - Latin, meaning "little plum"

Names for Boys
1. Parker - English name meaning "park keeper"
2. Phoenix - Greek name meaning "dark red"
3. Pierce - Welsh name meaning "son of Harry"
4. Paxton - English name meaning "peaceful town"
5. Princeton - English name meaning "prince's town"
6. Porter - English name meaning "doorkeeper"
7. Percy - English name meaning "pierce the vale"
8. Princeton - English name meaning "prince's town"
9. Prince - English name meaning "royal son"
10. Park - English name meaning "enclosed meadow"

Baby Names Beginning with "Q"

Names for Girls

1. Queenie - English, meaning "queen"
2. Qadira - Arabaic, meaning "powerful"
3. Qwynn - Gaelic, meaning "gift of the gab"
4. Quetzali - Nahuatl, meaning "precious thing"
5. Quirita - Spanish, meaning "spear"
6. Quanda - American, meaning "companion"
7. Qiao - Chinese, meaning "pretty" or "charming"
8. Quintessa - Latin, meaning "fifth born"
9. Quenilda - German, meaning "valiant"
10. Quetzalli - Aztec, meaning "precious feather" or "beautiful"

Names for Boys

1. Quinn - Irish name meaning "wise" or "counsel"
2. Quillan - Irish name meaning "cub"
3. Quill - English name meaning "feather pen"
4. Quentin - Latin name meaning "fifth"
5. Qasim - Arabic name meaning "divider" or "distributor"
6. Quaid - Irish name meaning "wise and clever"
7. Qiu - Chinese name meaning "Autumn" or "fall"
8. Quiron - German name meaning "wise centaur"
9. Quincy- French name meaning "estate of the fifth son"
10. Quay - English name meaning "wharf" or "dock"

Baby Names Beginning with "R"

Names for Girls

1. Renee - French, meaning "reborn"
2. Rayna – Hebrew, meaning "song of the Lord"
3. Regina - Latin, meaning "queen"
4. Rosalind - Spanish, meaning "pretty rose"
5. Rani - Hindu, meaning "queen"
6. Ramona - Spanish, meaning "wise protector"
7. Rhea - Greek, meaning "flowing" or "streaming"
8. Romy - German, meaning "rosemary"
9. Reva - Sanskrit, meaning "one who moves"
10. Ramona - Spanish, meaning "wise protector"

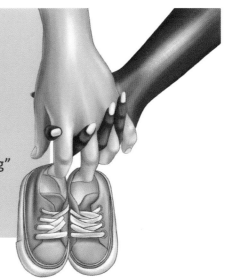

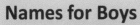

Names for Boys

1. Rowan - Irish name meaning "little red-haired one"
2. Ronan - Irish name meaning "little seal"
3. Riley - Irish name meaning "courageous"
4. Reece - Welsh name meaning "enthusiasm"
5. Rhett - Welsh name meaning "enthusiastic"
6. Roman - Latin name meaning "citizen of Rome"
7. Rohan - Indian name meaning "ascending"
8. Ransom - English name meaning "son of Rand"
9. Remington - English name meaning "place at the river's mouth"
10. Reagan - Irish name meaning "little king"

Baby Names Beginning with "S"

Names for Girls

1. Sadie - Hebrew, meaning "princess"
2. Skylar - Dutch, meaning "scholar"
3. Stella – Lattin, meaning "star"
4. Selena - Greek, meaning "goddess of the moon"
5. Sasha - Russian, meaning "defender of mankind"
6. Samira - Arabic, meaning "pleasant companion" or "entertaining friend"
7. Shiloh - Hebrew, meaning "tranquil" or "peaceful"
8. Serenity - English, meaning "peaceful" or "calm"
9. Samara - Hebrew, meaning "protected by God"
10. Safiya - Swahili, meaning "pure"

Names for Boys

1. Sawyer - English name meaning "one who cuts timber"
2. Shane - Irish name meaning "God is gracious"
3. Sterling - English name meaning "of high quality"
4. Sebastian - Latin name meaning "venerable"
5. Sullivan - Irish name meaning "dark-eyed"
6. Spencer - English name meaning "administrator of supplies"
7. Simon - Hebrew name meaning "to hear"
8. Silas - Latin name meaning "of the forest"
9. Sterling - English name meaning "of high quality"
10. Sullivan - Irish name meaning "dark-eyed"

Baby Names Beginning with " T "

Names for Girls

1. Tahira - Arabic, meaning "pure" or "chaste"
2. Tawana - Native American, meaning "a little one"
3. Tariro - Shona, meaning "hope"
4. Temitope - Yoruba, meaning "thanks be to God"
5. Thando - Xhosa, meaning "love"
6. Tilda - German, meaning "powerful in battle"
7. Thea – Greek, meaning "goddess"
8. Tilly – German, meaning "mighty in battle"
9. Trinity - Latin, meaning "threefold""
10. Thomasina - Aramaic, meaning "twin"

Names for Boys

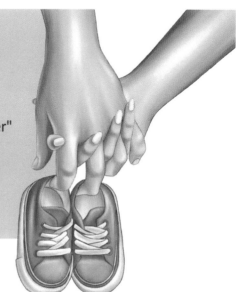

1. Tate - English name meaning "cheerful"
2. Theodore - Greek name meaning "gift of God"
3. Tucker - English name meaning "cloth maker"
4. Tate - English name meaning "cheerful"
5. Thatcher - English name meaning "roof thatcher"
6. Tiberius - Latin name meaning "of the Tiber"
7. Troy - Irish name meaning "foot soldier"
8. Tate - English name meaning "cheerful"
9. Tristan - Celtic name meaning "roof thatcher"
10. Tiberius - Latin name meaning "of the Tiber"

Baby Names Beginning with "U"

Names for Girls

1. Uma - Sanskrit, meaning "tranquillity" or splendour"
2. Una - Irish, meaning "one" or "unique"
3. Unity - English, meaning "oneness" or "harmony"
4. Ursula - Latin, meaning "little bear"
5. Uyen - Vietnamese, meaning "gentle, soft spoken"
6. Umaiza - Arabic, meaning "bright, shining star"
7. Uriela - Hebrew, meaning "God is my light"
8. Ushasree - Sanskrit, meaning "beauty of dawn"
9. Umiko - Japanese, meaning "child of the sea"
10. Ulani - Hawaiian, meaning "cheerful"

Names for Boys

1. Ulysses - Latin name meaning "wrathful"
2. Uriah - Hebrew name meaning "God is my light"
3. Upton - English name meaning "upper town"
4. Umberto - Italian name meaning "famous for brightness"
5. Ulf - Scandinavian name meaning "wolf"
6. Unwin - English name meaning "friend of the army"
7. Urban - Latin name meaning "from the city"
8. Ulrich - German name meaning "prosperous ruler"
9. Udale - English name meaning "valley of yew trees"
10. Uli - Hawaiian name meaning "chief"

Baby Names Beginning with "V"

Names for Girls

1. Valentina - Latin, meaning "strong, healthy"
2. Vida - Spanish, meaning "life"
3. Vianne - French, meaning "alive"
4. Vera - Russian, meaning "faith"
5. Vina - Hindi, meaning "musical instrument"
6. Vesper - English, meaning "evening"
7. Vuyelwa – South African, meaning "be happy"
8. Vero - Luo Kenyan, meaning "to sow"
9. Vimbai - Shona Zimbabwe, meaning "being diligent"
10. Verene - Latin, meaning "true, genuine"

Names for Boys

1. Vincent - Latin name meaning "conquering"
2. Vale - English name meaning "dweller in the valley"
3. Vance - English name meaning "marshland"
4. Van - Dutch name meaning "of"
5. Viggo - Scandinavian name meaning "warrior"
6. Vittorio - Italian name meaning "conqueror"
7. Vincent - Latin name meaning "conquering"
8. Vale - English name meaning "dweller in the valley"
9. Vance - English name meaning "marshland"
10. Van - Dutch name meaning "of"

Baby Names Beginning with "W"

Names for Girls

1. Willow - English, meaning "grace and flexibility"
2. Wanda - German, meaning "wanderer"
3. Wallis - English, meaning "foreigner"
4. Wanjiku – Kikuyu Kenya, meaning "born during the dry season"
5. Wudja - Egyptian, meaning "unite, join together"
6. Waziri - Swahili, meaning "minister, leader"
7. Wendo - Kikuyu, meaning "love"
8. Winta - Eritrean, meaning "winter"
9. Wura - Yoruba, meaning "gold"
10. Wafula – Luhya Kenya, meaning "born during the rainy season"

Names for Boys

1. Wyatt - English name meaning "brave in war"
2. Wai - Hawaiian name meaning "water"
3. Winston - English name meaning "joyful stone"
4. Walker - English name meaning "cloth walker"
5. Wilder - English name meaning "untamed"
6. Will - English name meaning "resolute protector"
7. West - English name meaning "from the west"
8. Wayne - English name meaning "wagon maker"
9. Wolfgang - German name meaning "traveling wolf"
10. Warren - English name meaning "enclosed land"

Baby Names Beginning with "X"

Names for Girls

1. Xanthe - Greek, meaning "yellow" or "blonde-haired"
2. Xenia - Greek, meaning "hospitality" or "welcoming"
3. Ximena - Spanish, meaning "hearkening" or "listener"
4. Xiomora - Spanish, meaning "ready for battle" or "warrior princess"
5. Xandra - Greek, meaning "defender of mankind"
6. Xyla - Greek, meaning "woodland"
7. Xinyi - Chinese, meaning "happy art"
8. Xoliswa - Xhosa South Africa, meaning "peaceful"
9. Xoey - Greek, meaning "life"
10. Ximene – Equatorial Guinea, meaning "one who listens"

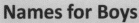

Names for Boys

1. Xavier - Basque name meaning "new house" or "bright"
2. Xander - Greek name meaning "defender of mankind"
3. Xenon - Greek name meaning "stranger"
4. Xanthe - Greek name meaning "yellow" or "fair hair"
5. Xavion - American name, a variant of Xavier
6. Xzander - Americanized version of Xander
7. Xylon - Greek name, meaning "from the forest"
8. Xadrian - Americanized version of Adrian
9. Xzavier - Americanized version of Xavier
10. Xylander - Americanized version of Alexander

Baby Names Beginning with " Y "

Names for Girls
1. Yaraa - Arabic, meaning "small butterfly"
2. Yasmine - Arabic, meaning "jasmine flower"
3. Yoko - Japanese, meaning "positive child"
4. Yuliana - Latin, meaning "youthful"
5. Yonina - Hebrew, meaning "dove"
6. Yen - Vietnamese, meaning "peaceful"
7. Yuliya - Russian, meaning "youthful"
8. Yagmur - Turkish, meaning "rain"
9. Ysadora - Greek, meaning "gift of Isis"
10. Yasma - Arabic, meaning "fragrant flower"

Names for Boys
1. Yale - Welsh name meaning "fertile upland"
2. York - English name meaning "from the yew tree estate"
3. Yves - French name meaning "yew tree"
4. Yates - English name meaning "gatekeeper"
5. Yorick - English name meaning "forever powerful"
6. Yardley - English name meaning "enclosed meadow"
7. Yakov - Hebrew name meaning "supplanter"
8. Yair - Hebrew name meaning "God will enlighten"
9. Yael - Hebrew name meaning "mountain goat"
10. Yusuf - Arabic name meaning "God increases"

Baby Names Beginning with " Z "

Names for Girls

1. Zaria - Nigerian, meaning "princess"
2. Zuri - Swahili, meaning "beautiful"
3. Zola - Latin, meaning "earth"
4. Zinnia - Latin, meaning "flower"
5. Ziva - Hebrew, meaning "brilliance" or "radiance"
6. Zelie - French, meaning "zealous"
7. Zuleika – Arabic, meaning "brilliant beauty"
8. Zofia - Polish, meaning "wisdom"
9. Zareen - Persian, meaning "golden"
10. Zaida - Arabic, meaning "abundance" or "prosperity"

Names for Boys

1. Zachary - Hebrew name meaning "God remembers"
2. Zane - English name meaning "God is gracious"
3. Zarek - Polish name meaning "protector"
4. Zander - Greek name meaning "defender of mankind"
5. Zackary - English variant of Zachary
6. Zephyr - Greek name meaning "west wind"
7. Zion - Hebrew name meaning "highest point" or "sign"
8. Zane - English name meaning "God is gracious"
9. Zakai - Hebrew name meaning "pure"
10. Zidan - Arabic name meaning "increase" or "growth"

For my beautiful baby,
Be you Boy or Girl!
I'll choose a name for you ,
Much more special than rubies or pearls!
You truly deserve to receive the very best,
A name that is different, unique from the rest!

The End

A good name is better than riches.
African Proverb